Quokkas mostly eat grass and the leaves of other small plants. They feed primarily on the ground, but they can climb low bushes to reach tasty twigs and leaves. Special bacteria that live in a quokka's stomach help the animal digest the tough plant fibers on which it relies for its daily food supply.

Quokkas feed mainly at nighttime, when the temperatures are coolest. During the day, they rest under trees and in other shady spots. Sometimes, male quokkas fight over who gets the best resting places. Each winner shares his shady spot with several females.

QUOKKAS FEED MOSTLY ON GRASS AND LEAVES THAT THEY FIND ON THE GROUND.

The largest concentration of quokkas is found on Rottnest Island, off the southwest coast of Australia. The island was given its name by a Dutch explorer who stepped ashore in 1696. He thought the quokkas were giant rats, so he named the island Rottnest, which means "rat's nest" in Dutch.

Small groups, or colonies, of quokkas also live on Bald Island and in a few swampy places on the southwestern Australian mainland.

ROTTNEST ISLAND WAS SO NAMED BECAUSE AN EXPLORER THOUGHT QUOKKAS WERE LARGE RATS.

The areas where quokkas live are also home to other kinds of animals. Rottnest Island, for example, is home to a great variety of birds. The island's salt lakes are populated by ducks,

Indian Ocean

Coral Sea

Australia

Rottnest
Island

WHERE
QUOKKAS
ARE FOUND

A quokka is about the size of a house cat. It averages 18 inches (45 centimeters) in length and weighs about 7 pounds (3.2 kilograms). It has a thick coat of coarse brownish-gray fur. Its small, round ears are set on top of its head and are almost hidden in the fur.

Like large kangaroos, the quokka has short front limbs and longer, more powerful back legs, which are used to hop from place to place. A large kangaroo has a strong tail that is used as a balance when the animal leaps across the land. A quokka's tail, however, is thin and not strong enough to act as a balance.

QUOKKAS HAVE SHORT
FRONT LIMBS AND
POWERFUL BACK LEGS.

Australia's first human inhabitants were a people called the Aborigines. It was the Aborigines who gave the name "quack-a" to the small, furry animal they saw roaming the land. Another name for a quokka is short-tailed scrub wallaby. That name is based on an Aborigine word, too. Wallabies are small kangaroos. The quokka is one of the smallest of them all.

The quokka has a scientific name, too: *Setonix brachyurus*. This name comes from Latin and Greek words meaning "stiff hair, short tail." This describes two obvious characteristics of quokkas.

AUSTRALIA'S EARLIEST NATIVE PEOPLE—THE ABORIGINES—GAVE THE QUOKKA ITS NAME.

All kangaroos, including quokkas, belong to a group of mammals called marsupials. Opossums, koalas, and a dog-like animal known as the Tasmanian devil are other kinds of marsupials.

The name *marsupial* means "having a pouch." Female marsupials give birth to tiny babies that are not completely developed. These babies finish their development within a fold or pouch of skin on the mother's belly. There, they feed on milk produced by the mother's mammary glands.

KANGAROOS, LIKE QUOKKAS, ARE
MARSUPIALS—ANIMALS WITH
POUCHES FOR THEIR YOUNG.

A QUOKKA IS A KIND OF KANGAROO.

A quokka is a shy animal that looks like a big, furry rat. Actually, it is a kind of kangaroo. When a quokka is in a hurry, it hops, just like other kangaroos. And like all other kangaroos, it is native to Australia.

What does it look like?

Where does it live?

What does it eat?

How does it reproduce?

How does it survive?

TURN THESE PAGES AND FIND OUT!

Published by Blackbirch Press, Inc.
260 Amity Road
Woodbridge, Connecticut 06525

©1997 Blackbirch Press, Inc.
First Edition

Printed in the United States of America

10 9 8 7 6 5 4 3 2 1

Photo Credits

Cover, title page: ©John Cancalosi/Peter Arnold, Inc.
Page 5: ©John Cancalosi/Peter Arnold, Inc.; page 7: ©Richard Kolar/Animals Animals; pages 8—9: ©Hans & Judy Beste/Animals Animals; page 11: ©John Cancalosi/Peter Arnold, Inc.; pages 12—13: ©A. B. Joyce/Photo Researchers, Inc.; page 15: ©K. G. Preston-Mafham/Animals Animals; pages 16—17: ©M. P. Kahl/Photo Researchers, Inc.; page 17 (inset): ©Tom McHugh/Photo Researchers, Inc.; page 18: ©John Cancalosi/Peter Arnold, Inc.; page 21: ©M. A. Chappell/Animals Animals; pages 22—23: ©Alan Foley/Animals Animals; page 25: ©Lindgren/Photo Researchers, Inc.; page 26: ©John Cancalosi/Peter Arnold, Inc.; page 29: ©K. G. Preston-Mafham/Animals Animals.
Map by Blackbirch Graphics, Inc.

Library of Congress Cataloging-in-Publication Data

Tesar, Jenny E.
What on earth is a quokka? / by Jenny Tesar. — 1st edition.
   p.   cm. — (What on earth series)
   Includes bibliographical references (p.   ) and index.
   ISBN 1-56711-104-1 (lib. bdg.: alk. paper)
   1. Quokka—Juvenlile literature. [1. Quokka]
I. Title. II. Series.
QL737.M35T47   1997
599.2—dc20   95-43327
                                    CIP
                                     AC

33,528 ✕

WHAT ON EARTH IS A
Quokka

?

JENNY TESAR

A BLACKBIRCH PRESS BOOK
WOODBRIDGE, CONNECTICUT

avocets, plovers, and stilts. Ospreys nest on steep cliffs. In spring, rock parrots and rainbow bee eaters fly over from the Australian mainland to lay eggs and raise their young.

On Rottnest Island, the quokkas' main enemy is the weather. Changing weather causes many important differences in winter and summer living conditions. During the winter, temperatures are mild and there is plenty of rain. The quokkas have enough water to drink and nutritious plants to eat. But summers are hot and dry. During this time, the healthiest plants for quokkas die because there is little or no water.

MANY PLANTS DRY OUT AND DIE DURING THE HOT SUMMERS ON ROTTNEST ISLAND.

Quokkas have several adaptations that help them live through hot, dry weather. One way is to gather at soaks, which are places along the edges of salt lakes. There, fresh water oozes from the ground. By digging into the soil, the quokkas can find a little water to drink. Quokkas also know how to find and eat the kinds of plants that contain stored water.

To keep cool and conserve water in their bodies, quokkas stay in shaded places during the day. They also lick themselves in order to stay more comfortable; as the water evaporates from their fur, the body is cooled. Quokkas cannot lick themselves too much, however, because that would make them too thirsty!

SHADE IS IMPORTANT TO QUOKKAS. IT HELPS THEM CONSERVE THE WATER IN THEIR BODIES.

To survive as a species, quokkas must reproduce. Reproduction is the process of making more organisms of the same kind. Without the act of reproduction, quokkas—or any other living thing—would die out, or become extinct.

As is true with most living things, quokka reproduction involves two parents. The male parent produces cells called sperm. The female parent produces an egg cell. A sperm and an egg join together to form one cell, called the fertilized egg. This cell divides many times and develops into a baby quokka.

The first step in quokka reproduction is mating. During mating, a male quokka fertilizes a female's egg.

Quokkas on Rottnest Island mate only after the hot, dry summer has ended. This means that the females will give birth and raise their babies while there is plenty of food to eat.

MALES AND FEMALES ARE
NEEDED FOR REPRODUCTION.

For a short time, the fertilized egg develops within the mother quokka's body. After only 27 days, a tiny, "premature" baby is born. It is blind, hairless, and not completely formed. It is also extremely tiny, weighing less than 0.03 ounce (about 1 gram).

The baby's only well-developed structures are the claws on its front paws. Using these claws, the baby climbs into its mother's pouch. There, it grips onto a nipple with its mouth. The nipple expands inside the mouth, so that the baby cannot be pulled loose until it is much older and better developed.

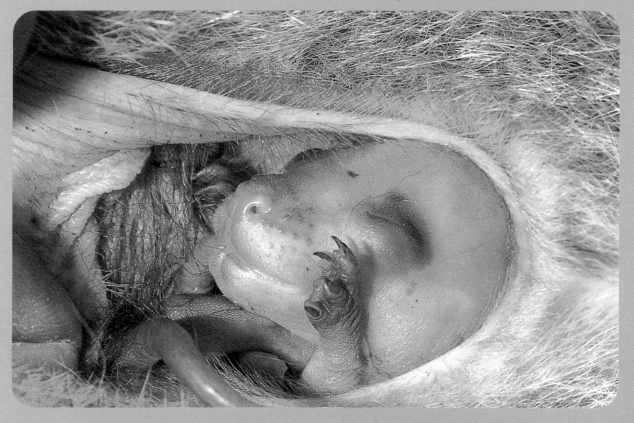

A DEVELOPING QUOKKA ATTACHES TO ITS MOTHER'S NIPPLE AS IT
GROWS INSIDE HER POUCH.

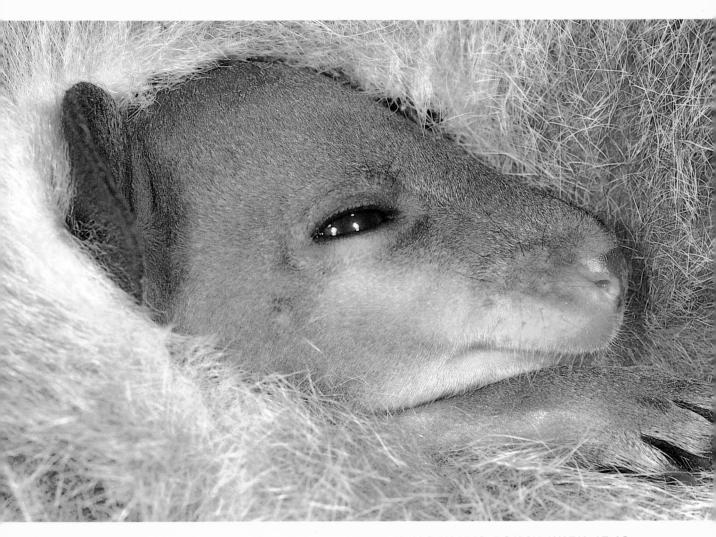

A YOUNG JOEY WILL REMAIN IN ITS MOTHER'S POUCH UNTIL IT IS ABOUT SEVEN MONTHS OLD.

A baby quokka is called a joey—this is the name for all baby kangaroos. It does not leave its mother's pouch until it is about seven months old. Then it begins to explore the world. But for several more months, the joey returns to its mother's pouch to rest, feed, and keep warm. By the time the joey is ten months old, it is too big to fit in the pouch. This means it is ready to live on its own.

Quokkas are very popular with people who visit Rottnest Island. Visitors enjoy watching these friendly little animals, which are quite tame.

The Australian government has passed laws that protect the quokkas on Rottnest Island. The laws are similar to those that protect animals in national parks. Australians realize that without quokkas, which are unique to their land, the world would be a much less interesting place.

QUOKKAS ARE TAME AND
QUITE FRIENDLY TO HUMANS.

Glossary

Pronunciation: Kwa•ka

adaptation A characteristic that helps a quokka to survive in its environment.

colony A group of animals that live together.

extinct No longer in existence.

fertilization The joining of a male sex cell, called a sperm, and a female sex cell, called an egg. Fertilization is a part of reproduction.

habitat The natural environment in which an organism lives.

joey A baby quokka or kangaroo.

marsupials Mammals that have a pouch on the stomach of the female; babies are fed and carried in the pouch.

reproduction Making more creatures of the same kind. When quokkas reproduce, they create baby quokkas.

soak A location where fresh water oozes from the ground.

Further Reading

Barrett, Norman. *Kangaroos and Other Marsupials.* New York: Franklin Watts, 1991.

Confort, Kellie. *A Picture Book of Australian Animals.* Mahwah, NJ: Troll, 1992.

Ganeri, Anita. *Small Mammals.* Chicago: Watts, 1993.

Lambert, David. *The Golden Concise Encyclopedia of Mammals.* New York: Western Publishing, 1992.

Parsons, Alexandra. *Amazing Mammals.* New York: Random House, 1990.

The Sierra Club Book of Small Mammals. San Francisco: Sierra, 1993.

Stanley-Baker, Penny. *Australia: On the Other Side of the World.* Ossining, NY: Young Discovery Library, 1988.

Stone, Lynn. *Kangaroos.* Vero Beach, FL: Rourke Corporation, Inc., 1990.

Tesar, Jenny. *Mammals.* Woodbridge, CT: Blackbirch Press, Inc., 1993.

Index